Katrina Katen, Psy.D.

The Ownership Yard

Where You Will Find True and
Lasting Happiness

INNER COMPASS

Inner Compass Publishing

Grand Junction, Colorado

Cover Design by CreateSpace

Cartoon Illustrations by Andrew Katen

Published by:
Inner Compass Publishing
420 North 8th Street
Grand Junction, CO 81501
www.myinnercompass.org

Inner Compass
420 North 8th Street
Grand Junction, CO 81501

Printed in the United States of America

ISBN-13:
978-0692326374 (Inner Compass)

ISBN-10:
0692326375

Dedication

To my beautiful family.

May you have clean yards, joyous hearts, and magnificent gardens!

Preface

"The Ownership Yard" was developed out of my work with adults, kids, teens, couples, and families. It proved to be a useful foundation for guiding each individual to develop healthy relationships and a clear sense of self. I soon discovered that the basic principles of the "Yard" transcend the four walls of the therapy room.

The goal of this book is not to solve every conceivable problem, heal every wound, or provide oversimplified advice that invalidates or minimizes the complexities of the human experience. Instead, the goal is to provide a framework for creating and experiencing true and lasting happiness.

Table of Contents

The Basics

Emotions

Relationships

End Note from the Author

Chapter 1
The Ownership Yard

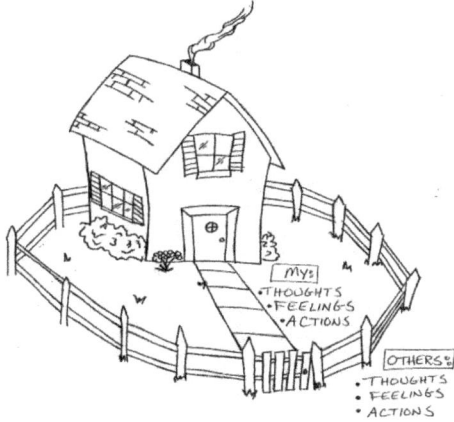

There are three things in your life that you have total control over and, thus, "own."

You own *your*:

1. Thoughts
2. Feelings
3. Actions

You do not (and cannot) own *others'*:

1. Thoughts
2. Feelings
3. Actions

Makes sense, right? Easy enough.

At the beginning of this chapter is a drawing of a house. Imagine you are the house.

Only what you can control is in your yard. In your yard are your thoughts, feelings, and actions. These are the three things in life that you truly own. No one can steal them. No one can use them. No one can borrow, destroy, or control them. Because you own your thoughts, feelings, and actions, you also own the consequences – both good and bad.

Outside your yard are other people's thoughts, feelings, and actions. Who owns other people's thoughts, feelings, and actions? You got it! They do. Everyone owns their thoughts, feelings, and actions, as well as the consequences – both good and bad. You cannot own other people's thoughts, feelings, and actions. You cannot steal them. You cannot borrow them. You cannot destroy them. And, you cannot control them.

This is "The Ownership Yard." It is natural law. It is true all the time, without exception. You can try to deny it, but you cannot defy it. Let's consider another natural law: gravity. Although you seemingly defy it when flying in an airplane, the law of gravity is always in effect. It takes a lot of fuel (energy) to counter gravity, and sooner or late you will run out of fuel. You will eventually drain your energy. You will eventually crash and burn. In the end, gravity (like ownership) always triumphs.

You may be thinking, "I own my things (car, house, furniture, toys, etc.), too." Technically, you do own your things – but you cannot fully control them. Your things can be stolen, borrowed, used, given up, and lost. Therefore, they are not in "The Ownership Yard."

Challenge

Draw yourself as a house.

Draw a fence around your house.

In your yard, list the 3 things you own. Outside of your
yard, list the 3 things you cannot own.

Post this drawing somewhere you can see it every day.

Chapter 2
Why It Matters

Thoughts, feelings, and
actions are central to every aspect of life.

Yours go wherever you go.

Anytime you attempt to put
someone else's thoughts, feelings,
or actions in your own yard, or put yours in
theirs, dis-ease is experienced. In turn, when you are able
to keep your yard clean, you will find, create, and
experience peace, joy, and all things that bring you
happiness.

The idea that one can only control his own thoughts,
feelings, and actions is not a new idea. "The Ownership
Yard" is merely a different way of understanding and
implementing this concept successfully. It nicely lends
itself to a phrase that I hope you soon find yourself saying:

"That's not in my yard."

There is a lot of freedom that comes from embracing this
phrase! Happiness awaits!

Challenge

What is an example of something in your life that does not include thoughts, feelings, or actions?

(Hint: there isn't one—this was a trick question!)

Chapter 3
"Shoulds"

When you apply the word "should" to yourself (I "should" not be upset, or I "should" be more active, or I "should" dress a certain way), this is a red flag that indicates you have placed someone's thoughts (beliefs) or feelings in your yard.

When you apply the word "should" to someone else's life (they "should" work harder, or they "should" dress better, or they "should" get married), you are attempting to put your "stuff" in someone else's yard.

So which one are you? Whose yard are you "shoulding" in – yours or theirs, or both?

When you fail to live up to someone else's "shoulds", how do you feel? Anxious, depressed, a failure, angry? What kind of irrational thoughts and actions ensue?

When someone else fails to live up to your "shoulds", how do you feel? Angry, annoyed, hurt? What kind of irrational thoughts and actions ensue?

At the end of the day, when other people "should" in your yard or you "should" in theirs, does anyone feel good? Is anything really accomplished? Not likely. The end result is most often, if not always, conflict, hurt, disappointment, unnecessary grief, and/or ruined relationships.

Instead of going around "shoulding" in everyone else's yard, try focusing on cleaning out all the "shoulds" in yours. Happiness awaits!

Chapter 4

Let Your Garden Grow

The unfortunate outcome of allowing others' "stuff" into your yard is that it covers up your yard. And, when your yard is covered with "stuff," your garden cannot grow.

When you are preoccupied with controlling others' thoughts (beliefs), you forget to control your own. And because their thoughts are on top, yours get buried. In the same way, when you are trying to control others' feelings, you fail to control your own. Your feelings get buried, smothered, and tangled with theirs.

The saddest outcome is when "shoulds" cover a yard so completely that they smother the garden. When you allow what others think to dictate your choices and actions, your yard becomes so filled with their "stuff" that you can't find your own. When your garden is covered it cannot grow.

You probably are not aware of all the "shoulds" in your yard. Take a minute to reflect on your life. How often is a choice influenced by what you "should" do, rather than by what you believe in your heart? How often do you choose a path because you "should," and not because it feels right?

Your garden cannot grow to be magnificent while buried under the "shoulds" of others. Who knows better what your garden needs to grow – you or others? When your yard is clean, you will find that you know exactly how your garden grows; and what a beautiful garden it is!

Challenge

Find a quote that encourages you to be and embrace exactly who you are! Read it daily.

Here are a few of my favorites:

"To be yourself in a world that is constantly trying to make you something else is the greatest accomplishment."
— Ralph Waldo Emerson

"Always be a first rate version of yourself and not a second rate version of someone else."
— Judy Garland

"Be yourself – not your idea of what you think somebody else's idea of yourself 'should' be."
— Henry David Thoreau

"Be yourself; everyone else is already taken."
— Oscar Wilde

Chapter 5
Boundaries

The 3 principles for Setting Boundaries

1. Boundaries are set with actions, not words.
2. To set a healthy boundary, you change *your* behavior—
   not someone else's.
3. The fence around "The Ownership Yard" is the
   boundary between where your thoughts, feelings, and
   actions end and others' begin.

The word "boundary" is used in many different contexts.
A physical boundary is a line that marks where one thing

ends and another begins. An interpersonal boundary is a line that marks where one person ends and another begins.

Physical boundaries are easy to identify. Even if I am holding someone's hand, I can clearly and easily discern where my hand ends and the other person's begins. If I am standing on my back porch, I can see where my yard ends and my neighbor's begins.

Interpersonal boundaries – including thoughts, feelings, and actions – are not as easily identified and rarely honored consistently. The closer the relationship, the fuzzier the boundary appears. Despite the ambiguous nature of interpersonal boundaries, they are nonetheless essential to healthy living and healthy relationships.

Let's look at the three principles of boundaries.

1. <u>Boundaries are set with actions, not words</u>.

   There is a great saying: "We teach people how to treat us." When you set boundaries with your actions (not words), you teach people where your boundaries are. When you give warnings and attempt to set boundaries with words, you teach people that you are willing to violate your own boundary, which means there is no boundary at all.

2. <u>To set a healthy boundary, you change *your* behavior – not someone else's.</u>

   People usually get this one backwards. More often than not, people try to set a boundary by dictating someone else's actions. This just doesn't work because *their* actions are not in *your* yard.

   You cannot keep others from acting in whatever way they choose. You can only control your actions and your responses. (Note: taking no action at all also sets a boundary.)

3. <u>The fence around the Ownership Yard is the boundary between where your thoughts, feelings, and actions end and others' begin.</u>

Your thoughts, feelings, and actions are in your yard, and thus interpersonal boundaries are outlined by the fence around your yard. Boundaries are violated when people attempt to take ownership of the "stuff" in someone else's yard, or when people try to put their own "stuff" in someone else's yard. The closer the relationship, the more misplaced ownership is present. The more misplaced ownership, the more unhappiness and grief will be experienced.

A healthy boundary represents ownership of thoughts, feelings, and actions. If you are uncomfortable, sad, or dissatisfied with an interaction or pattern of interactions, a boundary has likely been violated. To change what dissatisfies you, you must take stock of – and *change* – the "stuff" in your yard. Happiness exists and thrives inside healthy boundaries.

What do your actions teach others about what you are willing to *do* and *not do*? What do your actions tell people about what are you willing to tolerate or not tolerate? What do your actions tell people about your yard?

Verbal Warnings

If you really need to give warnings or feel your position must be explained, rephrase your *warning* to an *ownable boundary*. Just be sure you are prepared to follow through on that ownable action!

Warning: Stop cheating at the game, or else I won't play with you.

Ownable Boundary: I play games with opponents who don't cheat.

Warning: Stop calling me at work or I am not going to take your calls anymore.

Ownable Boundary: I will take your call between the hours of 4 and 8pm on weekdays and on weekends.

Chapter 6

Serenity, Courage, and Wisdom

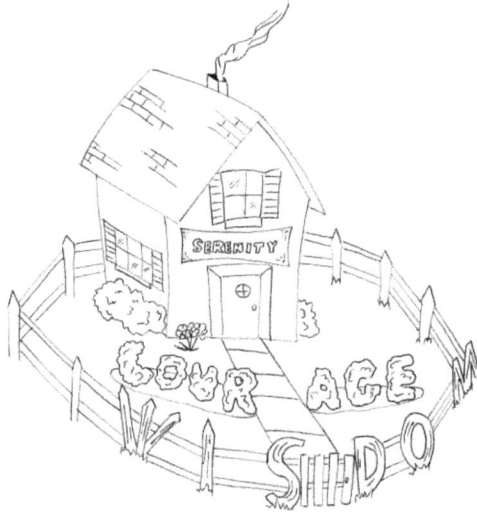

"Grant me the <u>serenity</u> to accept the things I cannot change, <u>courage</u> to change the things I can, and <u>wisdom</u> to know the difference."

Maybe you have heard this quote before? It is a good one! Let's take a closer look at its meaning and how it relates to "The Ownership Yard."

"<u>Serenity</u> to accept the things I cannot change."

> Serenity means "being peaceful." Peaceful means "free from disturbance." Grant me the freedom from the disturbance that comes with trying to control what I cannot change.
>
> Despite being unable to change, borrow, or control other people's thoughts, feelings, or actions, we

15

sure spend a good amount of time and energy trying. This futile effort leads to a host of negative feelings and wacky actions. Free yourself from these by finding serenity in the knowledge that you cannot own what is not yours.

"Courage to change the things I can."

Courage means having the strength to do something that frightens you. It means being brave. Taking ownership of your thoughts, feelings, and actions can be frightening because it means acknowledging that *you* control them, and that the consequences and outcomes (including your current situations/ circumstances and relationships) are your responsibility. That is scary! Looking at yourself – I mean *really looking at yourself* – is not easy to do, and it doesn't always reveal want you want to see.

On the flip side, the idea that you own your thoughts, feelings, and actions is empowering! You are not powerless and at the mercy of others. You are not a passenger. Instead, you are the driver. Finding courage means finding strength. And strength means power.

"Wisdom to know the difference."

Wisdom means having knowledge and good judgment. So how do you develop knowledge and good judgment about what you can change and what you cannot? The Ownership Yard! If it is your thought, feeling, or action, you can change it. If it is someone else's thought (belief or "should"), feeling, or action, you cannot change it.

Next time someone else's "should" finds its way into your yard (or you feel the urge to "should" in theirs by trying to rescue or control them), be wise, be courageous, and provide yourself serenity. Happiness awaits!

Chapter 7
The Meteor Headed for Earth

So far we have examined what is in your yard and what is in others' yards. Now I want to talk about the thing that is in no one's yard: the meteor headed for earth.

If there were a meteor headed for earth, there would be nothing you or I could do. It is not in your yard. It is not in mine. There are many things in life similar to that meteor: you did not cause it, someone else did not cause it, and we cannot remove ourselves from it.

Examples of "meteors" include some health issues (cancer, inability to have a child, genetic disorders, etc.), "big world" realities (taxes, war, elections, etc.), nature (natural disasters, weather changes, climate, etc.), and many, many more.

While these "meteors" are different from thoughts, feelings, and actions because they are not in anyone's yard, the natural law is the same: they are not in your yard. You can only control what is in your yard. Therefore, the way to handle "meteors" is the same:

Focus on what you can control (your thoughts, feelings, and actions), and control what you can.

Feelings
&
Emotions

Chapter 8
Guilt

Nearly everyone has experienced guilt. While people know it when they feel it, defining and resolving guilt often proves challenging, if not impossible.

Let's take a look at some formal definitions of guilt.

The following are taken from www.merriam-webster.com:

"Responsibility for a crime or for doing something bad or wrong."

"A bad feeling caused by knowing or thinking that you have done something bad or wrong."

Now let's examine these definitions through the lens of "The Ownership Yard." In this context, guilt can be divided into two types. The first type involves taking ownership over what is in your yard: "responsibility for a crime or for *doing* something bad or wrong" (emphasis added).

The second type is *misplaced ownership*: an attempt to own what is in someone else's yard. This type of guilt relates more closely to "a bad feeling," which may include dread, resentment, and confusion that results from a failed attempt to control someone else's thoughts and feelings.

Let's look at some examples of this second type of guilt:

1. It is your first pregnancy. You and your wife want to share the magical moment of seeing the beating heart together – just the two of you. But wait! Grandmother-to-be also wants to share in this precious moment. You gently tell her "no." Days later, you go to share the ultra sound pictures with her… and she begins to cry. "It must have been such a beautiful moment to hear the heartbeat for the first time, and I missed it," Grandma-to-be sobs. In that moment you feel it…Guilt! The voice in your head says, "I *should* have just let her be with us in that moment."

   With guilt there is always a "should" lurking in the shadows – and, healthy boundary setting is most often rewarded with a heavy dose of guilt!

2. It is that time of year: the annual family reunion and you are expected to attend. This same weekend you have been invited to participate in an exciting once-in-a-lifetime event at work. On the plane ride to the work event you receive a text with a picture of your grandpa grilling some hotdogs with the tag line: Wish you were here. Ugh! Guilt. (Can you find the hidden "should"?)

3. The gift of manipulation. Every year a distant cousin sends birthday and Christmas gifts. Every time – within three days of sending the gift – she emails your mother (remember, you are a grown adult) asking if you received the package. In true from, your mom insists you to send a thank-you card again. Your mom says, "Please send a thank-you – what am I going to say if I run into her and you have not acknowledged her thoughtfulness?"

   You feel guilty for not sending a thank-you card and for not sending a gift to her 6 kids for every birthday and holiday. At the same time you wish she would stop sending gifts because of the stress it causes. Then you feel guilty for not being grateful for the kindness and thoughtfulness. Then you feel angry because you feel you are being manipulated and "guilted" into engaging in this endless exchange of propriety and one-upmanship. Ugh! You think, "I need a personal assistant just to monitor and take care of all my 'shoulds!'" Then you wonder, "Maybe I should just start a file or a tracking system..." (What are the hidden "shoulds"? Hint: there are several here.)

4. You are exhausted and not feeling well due to an illness. Your close friend and biggest supporter is having a 50th wedding anniversary party and really, really wants you to be there. You are feeling so tired but do not want to hurt her feelings. If you don't go, you will feel guilty. If you do go, you know your body just can't handle it right now. (Whose yard are her feelings in? Whose yard is your good self-care in?)

5. You are an introvert. Every day a group of coworkers ask you to go to lunch. Here is the dilemma: Give yourself the needed mid-day recharge you desperately require to make it through the day, or give in because you don't want them to feel bad or believe you don't

like them. You say no thanks, and the coworker becomes offended and talks about you at lunch – Guilt! (Along with fear that you are not living up to what others think you "should" be and do). Maybe you can hear your voices whisper "Why can't I just be like everyone else and play nice in the sandbox?"

Removing the guilt from your yard is accomplished by identifying the "shoulds" lurking in the shadows. The dreaded feeling of guilt is a signal that you are running your life according to someone else's "shoulds" (code of conduct). Guilt results from the attempt to own others' feelings when you violate their "shoulds." Guilt is trying to own someone else's disappointment. *Guilt is misplaced ownership.*

Challenge

Reflect back on a time when you felt this dreaded guilt.

Look closely and find the "should" lurking in the shadows.

Now look closer. Where is the healthy boundary that has been violated? Your boundaries are important to resolving your guilt because your boundaries teach people how to treat you.

Chapter 9

Anxiety and Worry

Most people have been plagued by feelings of anxiety and worry at one time or another. Anxiety and worry can be like a shadow that follows you everywhere and blocks out the sun your garden needs to grow.

Anxiety and worry can be paralyzing, destructive, and prevent great things from coming to be. If you are a worrier, take a few minutes to reflect on what you worry most about. Here is a list of some very common worry thoughts:

1. What others think and say.
2. What my child's behavior says about my parenting.
3. What peers or coworkers saying about me after I walk by or leave the room?
4. My child's grades and future.
5. The safety of loved ones.
6. My health.
7. If I am going to be fired.
8. Public presentations or speaking in front of groups.

9. The economy.
10. The weather.
11. Is everyone having fun?

We can group these worries (and all others) into 4 categories:

1. What other people think.
2. What other people feel.
3. What other people do.
4. The meteor headed for earth.

We can group these four categories into one classification:

1. Outside your yard!

The things you worry about are outside your yard. Although you cannot control what is outside your yard, you still spend a great deal of energy trying. This is anxiety. *Anxiety is trying to control what is out of your control.* Like the fuel used to fly the airplane and defy gravity, the energy used trying to control what you cannot control eventually runs out...and you will crash and burn.

To resolve your anxiety and worry, you must sort out what you can control from what you cannot. Empowerment is the true "anti-anxiety." Focusing on what is in your yard is empowering because you have the power to control all that is in your yard.

Challenge

Identify something about which you worry or feel anxious.

Now do some yard work.

Chapter 10
Happiness

There is a great movie
(maybe you have seen it) called
The Wizard of Oz.

In this story Dorothy discovers
two things:

> 1. She has had the power all along (she did not need a wizard – and the wizard is merely a man behind a curtain).

> 2. "I know that if I ever go looking for my heart's desire, I'll never go any further than my own back yard. For if it isn't there, I never really lost it."

You have the power to create your own happiness because it is in your own back yard.

Creating Happiness is a two-step process:

1. First, clean out your yard by sorting out what you can control from what you cannot.
2. Once you have identified what you can control, identify and focus on *what you want* (in place of what you don't want).

Challenge

1. Pick an area of your life with which you are unhappy (work, marriage, health, etc.)
2. What can you control in this situation, and what can you not control?
3. List what makes you unhappy, or what you *don't* want.
4. Replace what you don't want with what you *do want*. For example, "I don't want to work 50 hours a week" can be changed to "I want to work four 10-hour days a week."

Relationships

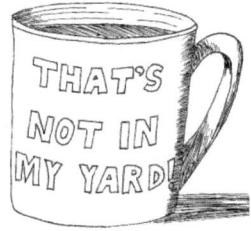

Chapter 11
The Workplace

There are some estimates that the average person spends 80,000 to 100,000 hours at work over the course of his life – that is more than 10 years! A full time employee devotes $5/7^{th}$ of the week to work. This is a lot of time!

Think of the times at work when you felt angry, resentful, betrayed, anxious, etc. Each of these negative emotions, as well as every negative interpersonal exchange, can be traced back to misplaced ownership.

A healthy workplace requires clean yards. The process of cleaning out your yard begins with the simple phrase, "That's not in my yard." (Of course, you may only want to say this phrase to yourself!)

There are four primary categories of relationships in the work place: (1) those you work for, (2) those who work for you, (3) those who work with you, and (4) the customer. Within each relationship (and in every single interaction) there are two yards: yours and theirs. What you can control remains the same: your thoughts, your feelings, and your actions. What you cannot control also remains the same: everything else.

Next time you feel resentful, hostile, angry, or anxious at work, ask yourself: "What am I trying to control that is not in my yard." Then remind yourself, "That's not in my yard."

Chapter 12
Family

"The family, that dear octopus from whose tentacles we never quite escape, nor in our innermost hearts never quite wish to."

– Dodie Smith

The biggest challenge when it comes to family is that one member's actions can greatly impact the whole family. For this reason, nowhere else on the planet will you find more misplaced ownership than within the family system. Many of our best and worst moments happen in the presence of our loved ones. As with any relationship, a healthy family system requires healthy boundaries. And healthy boundaries require ongoing yard work.

Healthy families have healthy gardens. Unhealthy families have unhealthy gardens. As with any relationship, you can only own what is yours. The most loving gift you can give is to own what is yours, and not try to own what is someone else's.

If you closely examine some of your family's most awful moments or painful conflicts, you will find misplaced ownership. Generally, you have to look very closely because the "shoulds" are deeply engrained and covert, and the spillage from one yard to another can be subtle.

Chapter 13
Children and Parenting

Parenting is a unique relationship. For most, the ultimate goal of parenting is to raise a child to become independent and mature. But what does it mean to be mature, and how do you know if you are? In relation to "The Ownership Yard," maturity means taking full ownership of one's thoughts, feelings, and actions.

Every child, regardless of age, has his own little yard with his own thoughts, feelings, and actions. If your parenting goal is to raise an independent and mature child, then you must guide the child to take full ownership of what he can control. This will never happen so long as you are owning (or trying to own) his "stuff." This will never happen as long as you are sending the message that it is okay for others to "should" in your child's yard. This will never happen as long as you model and reinforce misplaced ownership.

In most relationships, you teach people how to treat you. However, parent-child relationships are different. A child does not teach a parent how to treat him. Instead, the parent teaches the child *how he deserves to be treated*. The way you treat your child is how he comes to understand his value. You, as the parent, must never send the message that it is okay for anyone (including you) to "should" in your child's yard. And if someone tries to "should" in the child's yard, it is your job to provide the support and guidance necessary for the *child* to scoop it out of there. If your child's yard is filled with others' thoughts, feelings, and actions, his garden cannot grow.

You and your child have your own separate yards. This is not to say that each of you isn't greatly affected by the thoughts, feelings, and actions of each other. When your child hurts, you hurt. When your child is proud, you are proud. When your child is nervous, you are nervous. However, no matter how deeply you share his experiences and emotions, and no matter how badly you would like to, you cannot own what is not in your yard. Only your child can own what is in his yard. Only your child can resolve what is in his yard. And only your child can truly own the outcomes – both good and bad.

For a child, every opportunity to take ownership over his thoughts, feelings, and actions is an opportunity for self-esteem to develop, for confidence to build, and for his garden to grow!

When you ensure your child owns what is in his yard, you send a powerful message:

1. You are capable of handling it (whatever "it" may be).
2. Your garden is beautiful, let it grow!

Self-Inventory

Having an argument with your teen? What are you trying to own that you cannot?

Is meal time with your toddler an ongoing battle? What are you trying to own that is not yours?

Tips for Helping Your Child Keep A Clean Yard

✓ Model for the child by keeping your own yard clean.

✓ Help your child draw his ownership yard and explore what belongs and what does not.

✓ Support you child in embracing the phrase: "That is not in my yard."

✓ Support your child in taking ownership over his own thoughts, feelings, and actions by avoiding rescuing or solving his problems for him, and always validating his feelings, preferences, desires, and goals.

✓ Trust that your beautiful little creature has a wise body and wise mind that know exactly what he needs to have a beautiful and magnificent garden!

End Note from the Author

I hope you found the information in this book thought-provoking, useful, and inspiring! And if you did not like the book, well that's not in my yard. ☺

If you are moved to do some yard work, I encourage you to do so with courage, confidence, and most importantly humor. Maintain a playful spirit, find joy in all you do, and let your garden grow! May your yard be clean and your journey beautiful!

I want to conclude with one of my all-time favorite quotes:

"Dare to live the life you have dreamed for yourself. Go forward and make your dreams come true."
— Ralph Waldo Emerson

About the Author

Katrina Katen is a licensed psychologist with a doctoral degree in clinical psychology and master's degree with certification in marriage and family therapy. She is the owner of Individual Matters, LLC, a private practice that offers learning and psychological assessments; individual, child, family, and couples therapy; parent and couples workshops; professional development; and supervision/consultation. She also provides learning assessments and consultation through Inner Compass, an education and enrichment center.

Dr. Katen and her family live in the beautiful state of Colorado.

www.ingramcontent.com/pod-product-compliance
Lightning Source LLC
LaVergne TN
LVHW051818080426
835513LV00017B/2003